Bond
No.1 for exam success

SATs Skills

Reading Comprehension Workbook

10–11 years
Stretch

OXFORD
UNIVERSITY PRESS

Different types of question

You will find several different types of questions in this book:

- short answers which need one word or a few words
- several line answers which need one or two sentences
- longer answers where you need to explain in more detail, give several points and use evidence from the text.

Some questions have multiple-choice answers which may need ticking or circling. For some questions you may need to draw lines or complete a table.

Tips: Always look at the number of marks available and the amount of space provided for your answer. Use this as a guide to know how much to write.

If the question asks for evidence, make sure you include some short, relevant quotations from the text which help support your point.

Always use the text for evidence; do not rely on the pictures.

OXFORD
UNIVERSITY PRESS

Great Clarendon Street, Oxford, OX2 6DP, United Kingdom

Oxford University Press is a department of the University of Oxford.
It furthers the University's objective of excellence in research, scholarship, and education by publishing worldwide. Oxford is a registered trade mark of Oxford University Press in the UK and in certain other countries

British Library Cataloguing in Publication Data
Data available

978-0-19-274961-1

10 9 8 7 6 5 4 3 2 1

Paper used in the production of this book is a natural, recyclable product made from wood grown in sustainable forests. The manufacturing process conforms to the environmental regulations of the country of origin.

Printed in China

Acknowledgements

Cover illustration: Lo Cole

Page make-up and illustrations by Aptara

Extract from 'Experience: I flew the English Channel using a bunch of balloons' by Jonathan R Trappe, *Guardian Magazine*, 22 Jan 2011, copyright © Guardian News & Media Ltd 2011, 2016, reproduced by permission of GNM.

Although we have made every effort to trace and contact all copyright holders before publication this has not been possible in all cases. If notified, the publisher will rectify any errors or omissions at the earliest opportunity.

Chapter 1: The One Thing Needful

Read the passage below, then answer the questions that follow.

In this **extract** from the opening of Charles Dickens' novel *Hard Times*, the character Thomas Gradgrind is explaining his views on how children should be educated.

"Now, what I want is, Facts. Teach these boys and girls nothing but Facts. Facts alone are wanted in life. Plant nothing else, and root out everything else. You can only form the minds of reasoning animals upon Facts: nothing else will ever be of any service to them. This is the principle on which I bring up my own children, and this is the principle on which I bring up these children. Stick to Facts, sir!"   5

The scene was a plain, bare, monotonous vault of a school-room, and the speaker's square forefinger emphasized his observations by underscoring every sentence with a line on the schoolmaster's sleeve. The emphasis was helped by the speaker's square wall of a forehead, which had his eyebrows for its base, while his eyes found commodious cellarage in two dark caves, overshadowed   10 by the wall. The emphasis was helped by the speaker's mouth, which was wide, thin, and hard set. The emphasis was helped by the speaker's voice, which was inflexible, dry, and dictatorial. The emphasis was helped by the speaker's hair, which bristled on the skirts of his bald head, a plantation of firs to keep the wind from its shining surface, all covered with knobs, like the crust of a plum pie, as   15 if the head had scarcely warehouse-room for the hard facts stored inside. The speaker's obstinate carriage, square coat, square legs, square shoulders, – nay, his very neckcloth, trained to take him by the throat with an unaccommodating grasp, like a stubborn fact, as it was, – all helped the emphasis.

"In this life, we want nothing but   20
Facts, sir; nothing but Facts!"

The speaker, and the schoolmaster,
and the third grown person present,
all backed a little, and swept with
their eyes the inclined plane of little   25
vessels then and there arranged in
order, ready to have imperial gallons
of facts poured into them until they
were full to the brim.

(A) In the opening paragraph, what is the **main** message of Gradgrind's speech? [1]

Tick **one**.

Children should be seen and not heard. ☐

Children's minds are like animals. ☐

Being taught anything but facts will be useless in life. ☐

Teachers should always find out the facts. ☐

(B) Which words or **phrase** in the first paragraph tell the reader that Gradgrind is a father? [1]

_____

(C) What does the second paragraph suggest the schoolroom is like? [2]

_____

_____

(D) Thomas Gradgrind's forehead is compared to: [1]

Circle **one**.

a shadow   a cellar   a wall   a cave

(E) Circle the word that is **closest** in meaning to dictatorial, in the second paragraph. [1]

bossy   loud   low   clear

(F) Look at the description of Gradgrind's hair and head, starting from *The emphasis was helped by the speaker's hair...*

What does this tell you about Gradgrind's head? [3]

_____

_____

_____

_____

(G) *trained to take him by the throat with an unaccommodating grasp*

Explain what this tells you about how Gradgrind's neckcloth is tied. [1]

_____

(H) Using the information in paragraph two, explain what impression is created of Gradgrind. [3]

_____

_____

_____

_____

(I) How many adults are present in this extract? [1]

_____

(J) In the final paragraph, the children are referred to as *little vessels*. How does this phrase help the reader to understand Gradgrind's view of education? [2]

_____

_____

_____

(K) *In this life, we want nothing but Facts, sir; nothing but Facts!*

How does the way this line is written help to emphasis the meaning? [2]

_____

_____

_____

9

Behind the Curtains: Theatre Superstitions

Read the text below, then answer the questions that follow.

The world of theatre is full of superstitions. Perhaps this is unsurprising, since theatre has always had a connection with magic and the supernatural. In fact, some people feel that to produce good theatre is to create an illusion. Whatever the reasons behind it, it is true to say many of those who work on- or backstage still pay heed to these superstitions. Some beliefs and customs are well-known, **5** such as the perils of mentioning Shakespeare's play *Macbeth* by name. Others are more obscure – who knew that knitting backstage is believed to be unlucky? Here are just a few of the most intriguing ones:

Whistling: No whistling in theatres should ever be heard, according to custom. It is thought that this superstition came about during the time when out-of- **10** work sailors were often employed as extra stage hands, manoeuvring scenery and operating the early mechanical fly systems. These involved a series of ropes or rigging controlling wooden beams which lowered and raised different parts of the set. As sailors, the men would have been used to carrying out different instructions on board their ship, according to whistled commands. **15** Consequently, if someone whistled on stage, the sailor might interpret this as a signal to move the fly and cause a serious accident by dropping the scenery at the wrong point.

Lit candles: Never having more than two lit candles backstage is a superstition grounded in safety. Fires in theatres were common before the advent of **20** electricity, as the story below will testify, so it is hardly surprising that having three lit candles backstage is a theatre faux-pas. Nowadays there are strict health and safety laws about using any kind of naked flame in a theatre and a fire officer must always be present if candles are lit on stage, as well as a safety curtain which will often be lowered in the interval. **25**

> **Why do theatres have safety curtains?**
> A common misunderstanding amongst theatre audiences is that when the safety curtain comes down across the front of the stage, usually during the interval of a show, it is to prevent a potential fire spreading at that time. Although this has some truth in it, the primary reason is to check that the curtain is working in case it is needed at some point during the performance, **30**

rather like testing the fire alarms. Safety curtains, along with several other safety features in theatres, were introduced by law, after a catastrophic fire devastated the Theatre Royal in Exeter on 5 September 1887.

It was the first night of a play called Romany Rye *and an audience of 800 people had packed into the newly-built theatre, when the flame from a gas lamp ignited some drapes backstage. The number of escape routes and exits was limited and there was tragic loss of life – over 180 people died in the blaze, leading to calls for better building designs with adequate escape routes to be compulsory in all theatres. As electricity replaced gas lamps to provide lighting in theatres, safety improved.*

35

40

Yellow, green and blue: Costumes in these colours are said to bring misfortune to a production. Traditionally, yellow and green are said to be the colours of the devil and therefore should not be worn, to avoid negative associations. Blue is similarly unlucky – it would have been the most expensive colour to dye cloth in the early days of theatre and if a theatre company was running into financial difficulties, costumes made of blue fabric were often worn to try to convince audiences that they were doing well.

45

Flowers, mirrors and jewellery: All of these may be required on stage as props from time to time, but to use real ones is considered bad luck. Logic underpins the reasoning: real flowers wilt, real mirrors interfere with the lighting and real jewellery, which is likely to be valuable, may be stolen.

50

The ghost light: Visit a theatre when it is shut (or 'dark' as it is known) and you will usually find a light left on over the stage. This is often referred to as the 'ghost' light. Superstitious theatre people will tell you this is to allow the theatre ghosts opportunity to perform on stage when the theatre is empty, so that they do not interfere with the show itself, when the real actors are performing. Perhaps a more practical explanation is to ensure the person who is last out and first into the theatre does not trip over anything in the dark!

55

Whatever the history of these superstitions, it is clear that those who work in theatre today are not willing to risk the fortunes of their show by ignoring them any time soon!

60

by Christine Jenkins

(A) This article is entitled 'Behind the Curtains: Theatre Superstitions'. Find **two** other words in the first paragraph which are also used to mean a superstition. [2]

(B) Circle the word which is closest in meaning to the word *obscure* at the end of paragraph one. [1]

frightening   plausible   unusual   well-known

(C) Using the information in paragraph two, explain **in your own words** how the superstition involving whistling is thought to have originated. [2]

(D) How are theatres nowadays better protected against the risk of fire? Use information from the text box and paragraph three to find **three** ways. [3]

(E) *over 180 people died in the devastating blaze*

Which other words in the text about the Exeter fire show you that: [2]

many people died?

the theatre was destroyed?

(F) Give **two** possible beliefs about the origins of the 'ghost' light. [2]

_____

_____

(G) Read the following statements and tick whether they are facts or opinions. [1]

	Fact	Opinion
Safety curtains are tested regularly.		
Theatre is like magic.		
Sailors were employed to operate scenery.		
Knitting offstage brings bad luck.		

(H) Using information **from across the text**, complete the table. [3]

Custom	Likely reason
Blue costumes	
	Fire safety
Yellow and green costumes	
	Will die
Mirrors	

(I) Many theatre superstitions originated from historical facts or safety concerns. Explain how the text supports this view, using evidence from across the article. [3]

_____

_____

_____

_____

9

Experience: I Flew the English Channel Using a Bunch of Balloons

'Experience' is a weekly series of **autobiographical** articles in the *Guardian* newspaper, in which people write about an interesting or unusual experience they have had.

Read the passage below, then answer the questions that follow.

The idea came up during a conversation in the office. A colleague at the IT company where I work mentioned a story he'd seen about a failed attempt to fly using helium balloons. I said it had to be possible – that with enough of them I could make the chair I was sitting in fly. It was a typical Friday afternoon conversation and no one took it very seriously. But the idea stuck with me and kept nagging.   5

So I bought a few balloons – nothing unusual, just the big ones that are often used at displays and promotions – to see if I could get the chair to take off. With rigging, it took five balloons to get it airborne. That was a point of no going back – I knew the next step had to be to fly in the chair myself.

As children, I think, most of us imagine holding a balloon on a string and   10
drifting away. It crosses cultures and borders, but we're told it's impossible.
I enrolled at a flight school to become licensed to fly hot-air and gas balloons.
Then I worked out how many balloons I'd need, designed the rigging and safety harness. I did all the physics on paper, built models, and a year later was ready to make the inaugural flight.   15

That flight took place in June 2008. Strapped into my office chair under a canopy of 55 balloons, I covered more than 50 miles in four hours, climbing to an altitude of nearly 15 000 ft. Last April, I broke the world record for the longest free-floating balloon flight – a 14-hour journey across North Carolina. The record wasn't my goal. Really, I wanted to prove to myself that crossing the English   20
Channel was within my grasp.

I had to give it a shot. Of course, approaching the Civil Aviation Authority to register a cluster of balloons as an aircraft isn't easy. Then there was insurance, airworthiness inspections and so on, which took a lot of time and paperwork.

The night before the flight, in May last year, I was very afraid. The balloons had   25
to be inflated at night, so I could take off at sunrise when the wind is calmest.
There's something about the dead of night that adds to the feeling of dread. I'm
not a reckless adventurer and had planned scrupulously for the right weather,

but once airborne I could rely only on myself, minute to minute. The flight began 10 miles inland at a gliding club in Ashford. At 5 a.m., I simply floated away, gradually climbing over the Kent countryside. After all the work and the waiting, it was a relief to be free of the earth. **30**

By sheer luck, I hit the coast right at the white cliffs of Dover. As I drifted out over open water, the chair turned by chance through 360 degrees, giving me a spectacular view of the cliffs and the land receding as it did so. **35**

This form of flight is the only one that's truly silent. There are no jets, no rotors – with a hot-air balloon you have the sound of the flame, and even in a glider you hear the wind rushing past. Hanging from helium balloons, you're moving with the wind. You don't feel it on your skin – it's incredibly peaceful.

England was behind me, the cold waters of the channel lay below and it was **40** 41 miles to the continent. There were about a hundred potential problems I'd had to consider and prepare for. Boats and ships were few and far between, and I knew that sudden immersion in the cold water could kill me in minutes – I'd rejected the idea of using a wet suit to keep the weight down.

Yet the sheer joy of the adventure outweighed any fear. At the start of the **45** journey, I had to call air traffic control in London on my radio to open my flight plan – the delight of being able to announce, "London, this is gas balloon November 878 Uniform Papa" cannot be underestimated.

Descending from 7000 ft, I approached France, passing right over the lighthouse at Dunkirk. The bad news was, I was heading for the Belgian border, and I didn't **50** have permission to land there. Ahead of me were two radio towers – potentially deadly, as their guy wires can slice clean through the balloons. Needing to reach the ground quickly, I cut off a whole tier of my balloons and landed with a single bounce in a field full of lettuces.

The entire journey lasted three hours and 22 minutes. Compared with the exhaustive **55** preparation, it was nothing, but the feeling of accomplishment will last a lifetime.

Extract from 'Experience: I flew the English Channel using a bunch of balloons' by Jonathan R Trappe, *Guardian Magazine*, 22 January 2011.

(A) What was the *idea that came up during a conversation in the office*, in paragraph one? [1]

_____

(B) How does the **narrator**'s view of the idea differ from that of other people? [2]

_____

_____

(C) Which phrase is closest in meaning to the word *airborne* in the second paragraph? Circle the correct answer. [1]

Lighter than air   Flying with someone in it

High enough to fly   Lifted off the ground

(D) Which words, in paragraph three, suggest that most people could relate to this story? [1]

_____

(E) Using the information in paragraph three, describe **three** ways Jonathan Trappe prepared for the flight. [3]

_____

_____

_____

(F) What does the word *inaugural* mean, in paragraph three? Circle **one**. [1]

record-breaking   first

dangerous   impossible

G Reread paragraph four and match the following: [1]

Number of balloons lifting the chair	14 hours
Distance travelled in four hours	15 000 feet
Length of world record-breaking flight	55
Height above the ground reached	50 miles

H *The record wasn't my goal.*

What does this suggest about Jonathan Trappe's attitude towards the experience? [1]

_____

I Explain why the phrase *within my grasp*, at the end of paragraph four, is effective. [2]

_____

_____

J *Of course, approaching the Civil Aviation Authority to register a cluster of balloons as an aircraft isn't easy.*

Explain why this might not have been easy. **Refer to the text** in your answer. [2]

_____

_____

K Which words in paragraph six indicate that he was careful? Find **two** examples. [2]

_____

_____

L In paragraphs seven and eight, which aspects of the flight does he find enjoyable? [2]

_____

_____

10

(M) In paragraph nine, what is suggested by the sentence *There were about a hundred potential problems I'd had to consider and prepare for*? Circle **one**. [1]

He overcame lots of problems on the journey.

He did not think there would be any problems.

He hoped he wouldn't face hundreds of difficulties.

He had thought of all the possible difficulties.

(N) Reread paragraph 11. What problems did he face when landing? [2]

_____

_____

(O) How do the feelings of Jonathan Trappe towards his experience change throughout the article? **Refer to evidence** from the text to support your answer. [3]

_____

_____

_____

_____

Down the Rabbit Hole

Read the text below, then answer the questions that follow.

Alice was beginning to get very tired of sitting by her sister on the bank, and of having nothing to do: once or twice she had peeped into the book her sister was reading, but it had no pictures or conversations in it, "and what is the use of a book," thought Alice, "without pictures or conversations?"

So she was considering in her own mind (as well as she could, for the hot day made her feel very sleepy and stupid) whether the pleasure of making a daisy-chain would be worth the trouble of getting up and picking the daisies, when suddenly a White Rabbit with pink eyes ran close by her.   **5**

There was nothing so *very* remarkable in that; nor did Alice think it so very much out of the way to hear the Rabbit say to itself, "Oh dear! Oh dear! I shall be too late!" (when she thought it over afterwards, it occurred to her that she ought to have wondered at this, but at the time it all seemed quite natural); but when the Rabbit actually *took a watch out of its waistcoat-pocket*, and looked at it, and then hurried on, Alice started to her feet, for it flashed across her mind that she had never before seen a rabbit with either a waistcoat-pocket, or a watch to take out of it, and burning with curiosity, she ran across the field after it, and was just in time to see it pop down a large rabbit hole under the hedge.   **10**   **15**

In another moment down went Alice after it, never once considering how in the world she was to get out again.

The rabbit hole went straight on like a tunnel for some way, and then dipped suddenly down, so suddenly that Alice had not a moment to think about stopping herself before she found herself falling down what seemed to be a very deep well.   **20**

Either the well was very deep, or she fell very slowly, for she had plenty of time as she went down to look about her, and to wonder what was going to happen next. First, she tried to look down and make out what she was coming to, but it was too dark to see anything; then she looked at the sides of the well and noticed that they were filled with cupboards and book-shelves: here and there she saw maps and pictures hung upon pegs. She took down a jar from one of the shelves as she passed; it was labelled "ORANGE MARMALADE", but to her disappointment it was empty; she did not like to drop the jar for fear of killing somebody underneath, so managed to put it into one of the cupboards as she fell past it.   **25**   **30**

"Well!" thought Alice to herself. "After such a fall as this, I shall think nothing of tumbling down stairs! How brave they'll all think me at home! Why, I wouldn't say anything about it, even if I fell off the top of the house!" (Which was very likely true.)   35

Down, down, down. Would the fall *never* come to an end? "I wonder how many miles I've fallen by this time?" she said aloud. "I must be getting somewhere near the centre of the earth. Let me see: that would be four thousand miles down. I think – " (for, you see, Alice had learnt several things of this sort in her lessons in the schoolroom, and though this was not a *very* good opportunity   40 for showing off her knowledge, as there was no one to listen to her, still it was good practice to say it over) " – yes, that's about the right distance – but then I wonder what Latitude or Longitude I've got to?" (Alice had no idea what Latitude was, or Longitude either, but thought they were nice grand words to say.)

Presently she began again. "I wonder if I shall fall right *through* the earth!   45 How funny it'll seem to come out among the people that walk with their heads downwards! The Antipathies, I think – " (she was rather glad there *was* no one listening, this time, as it didn't sound at all the right word) " – but I shall have to ask them what the name of the country is, you know. Please, Ma'am, is this New Zealand or Australia?" (and she tried to curtsey as she spoke – fancy *curtseying*   50 as you're falling through the air! Do you think you could manage it?) "And what an ignorant little girl she'll think me! No, it'll never do to ask: perhaps I shall see it written up somewhere."

Down, down, down. There was nothing else to do, so Alice soon began talking again. "Dinah'll miss me very much tonight, I should think!" (Dinah was the   55 cat.) "I hope they'll remember her saucer of milk at tea-time. Dinah, my dear, I wish you were down here with me! There are no mice in the air, I'm afraid, but you might catch a bat, and that's very like a mouse, you know. But do cats eat bats, I wonder?" And here Alice began to get rather sleepy, and went on saying to herself, in a dreamy sort of way, "Do cats eat bats? Do cats eat bats?"   60 and sometimes, "Do bats eat cats?" for, you see, as she couldn't answer either question, it didn't much matter which way she put it. She felt that she was dozing off, and had just begun to dream that she was walking hand in hand with Dinah, and saying to her very earnestly, "Now, Dinah, tell me the truth: did you ever eat a bat?" when suddenly, thump! thump! down she came upon a heap of   65 sticks and dry leaves, and the fall was over.

Alice was not a bit hurt, and she jumped up on to her feet in a moment: she looked up, but it was all dark overhead; before her was another long passage,

and the White Rabbit was still in sight, hurrying down it. There was not a moment to be lost: away went Alice like the wind, and was just in time to hear it   70
say, as it turned a corner, "Oh my ears and whiskers, how late it's getting!" She was close behind it when she turned the corner, but the Rabbit was no longer to be seen: she found herself in a long, low hall, which was lit up by a row of lamps hanging from the roof.

There were doors all round the hall, but they were all locked; and when Alice had   75
been all the way down one side and up the other, trying every door, she walked sadly down the middle, wondering how she was ever to get out again.

Suddenly she came upon a little three-legged table, all made of solid glass; there was nothing on it but a tiny golden key, and Alice's first idea was that this might belong to one of the doors of the hall; but, alas! either the locks were too   80
large, or the key was too small, but at any rate it would not open any of them. However, on the second time round, she came upon a low curtain she had not noticed before, and behind it was a little door about fifteen inches high: she tried the little golden key in the lock, and to her great delight it fitted!

From *Alice's Adventures in Wonderland* by Lewis Carroll

Ⓐ What impression of Alice is created in paragraphs one and two? [2]

_____

_____

Ⓑ Reread paragraph three. Explain which aspects of the scene are *remarkable*. [2]

_____

_____

Ⓒ Circle the phrase which is closest in meaning to *flashed across her mind*. [1]

Had a good idea   Suddenly forgot something

Suddenly realised something   Had a headache

5

(D) Explain what the phrase *burning with curiosity* shows us about Alice and describe how her actions in paragraphs four and five reflect this. [2]

_____

_____

(E) How does the author convey the idea in paragraphs five to ten that Alice falls a long way down? [2]

_____

_____

(F) Which words in paragraph six show that Alice likes marmalade? [1]

_____

(G) How does the choice of language in paragraphs five to ten create an impression that falling down the rabbit hole was a strange but not unpleasant experience for Alice? **You should refer to: the sights inside the well itself and Alice's thoughts**. [3]

_____

_____

_____

(H) Alice mentions things she has learnt *in her lessons in the schoolroom* in paragraphs eight and nine. Find **two** examples of this. [2]

_____

_____

(I) What does the expression *alas!* suggest in paragraph 13? [1]

_____

11

Ⓙ Tick whether the following statements about Alice reaching the bottom of the tunnel are true or false. [1]

	True	False
She was hurt a little bit.		
She cannot see daylight.		
She has to go fast to keep up with the White Rabbit.		
She lands gently on the ground.		

Ⓚ How do Alice's feelings change over the course of this extract? [3]

_____

_____

_____

_____

Ⓛ This extract is part of the opening chapter of the book *Alice's Adventures in Wonderland*. Explain how this is a good title for the story so far. [3]

_____

_____

_____

Ⓜ Put these sentences into the correct order. The first one has been done for you. [1]

The White Rabbit disappears down a rabbit hole under the hedge. ☐

Alice finds a small key. ☐

Alice spots the White Rabbit above ground. 1

Alice thinks about her cat. ☐

Alice finds a marmalade jar. ☐

8

Why the Evergreen Trees Never Lose Their Leaves: A *Folk Tale*

Winter was coming, and the birds had flown far to the south, where the air was warm and they could find berries to eat. One little bird had broken its wing and could not fly with the others. It was alone in the cold world of frost and snow. The forest looked warm, and the little bird made its way to the trees as well as it could, to ask for help.

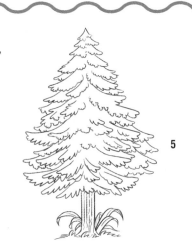

5

First it came to a birch tree. "Beautiful birch tree," it said, "my wing is broken, and my friends have flown away. May I live among your branches till they come back to me?"

"No, indeed," answered the birch tree, drawing her fair green leaves away. "We of the great forest have our own birds to help. I can do nothing for you."

10

"The birch is not very strong," said the little bird to itself, "and it might be that she could not hold me easily. I will ask the oak." So the bird said, "Great oak tree, you are so strong, will you not let me live on your boughs till my friends come back in the springtime?"

15

"In the springtime!" cried the oak. "That is a long way off. How do I know what you might do in all that time? Birds are always looking for something to eat, and you might even eat up some of my acorns."

"It may be that the willow will be kind to me," thought the bird, and it said, "Gentle willow, my wing is broken, and I could not fly to the south with the other birds. May I live on your branches till the springtime?"

20

The willow did not look gentle then, for she drew herself up proudly and said, "Indeed, I do not know you, and we willows never talk to creatures whom we do not know. Very likely there are trees somewhere that will take in strange birds. Leave me at once."

The poor little bird did not know what to do. Its wing was not yet strong, but it began to fly away as well as it could. Before it had gone far, a voice was heard. "Little bird," it said, "where are you going?"

25

"Indeed, I do not know," answered the bird sadly. "I am very cold."

"Come right here, then," said the friendly spruce tree, for it was her voice that had called. "You shall live on my warmest branch all winter if you choose."

30

"Will you really let me?" asked the little bird eagerly.

"Indeed, I will," answered the kind-hearted spruce tree. "If your friends have flown away, it is time for the trees to help you. Here is the branch where my leaves are thickest and softest."

"My branches are not very thick," said the friendly pine tree, "but I am big and strong, and I can keep the north wind from you and the spruce." 35

"I can help too," said a little juniper tree. "I can give you berries all winter long, and every bird knows that juniper berries are good."

So the spruce gave the lonely little bird a home, the pine kept the cold north wind away from it, and the juniper gave it berries to eat. 40

The other trees looked on and talked together wisely.

"I would not have strange birds on my boughs," said the birch.

"I shall not give my acorns away for any one," said the oak.

"I never have anything to do with strangers," said the willow, and the three trees drew their leaves closely about them. 45

In the morning all those shining green leaves lay on the ground, for a cold north wind had come in the night, and every leaf that it touched fell from the tree.

"May I touch every leaf in the forest?" asked the wind in its frolic.

"No," said the frost king. "The trees that have been kind to the little bird with the broken wing may keep their leaves." 50

This is why the leaves of the spruce, the pine and the juniper are always green.

Features of Folk Tales

Folk tales are stories that have been passed on by word of mouth, within a particular culture. Many have the following things in common:

- The characters are usually humans or animals with human characteristics.
- They frequently teach a **moral** or message that people can live by. 55
- Things often appear in threes.
- They may explain how something came into being.
- The main character may face a quest or challenge.
- They may feature characters with magic or supernatural powers.
- Good wins over evil. 60

(A) Why does the little bird need shelter? Give **two** reasons. [2]

_____

_____

(B) Compare how the birch tree and the oak tree are described by completing the table with words **from the text**. [1]

Birch	
Oak	

(C) *"In the springtime!" cried the oak. "That is a long way off. How do I know what you might do in all that time? Birds are always looking for something to eat, and you might even eat up some of my acorns."*

Explain how the oak tree felt about the bird's request. [1]

_____

(D) Reread the paragraph beginning 'The willow did not look gentle then…'

Describe **two** ways the willow shows she is not gentle, referring to the text in your answer. [2]

_____

_____

(E) As the first three trees reject the bird, describe how the bird may feel, **referring to the text** in your answer. [1]

_____

_____

(F) Describe the role of each of the three evergreen trees in helping the bird. [3]

Spruce	
Pine	
Juniper	

10

Answers

Unit 1

(A) Being taught anything but facts will be useless in life. [1]

(B) *my own children* [1]

(C) Refer to any two aspects: empty, *bare / plain*, dull / possibly dark with no windows (suggested by word *vault*) [2]

(D) a wall [1]

(E) bossy [1]

(F) Refer to three of the following: bald / bristles of hair around bald patch / hair sticks up / surface is shiny / surface is bumpy [3]

(G) tied very tightly, almost choking him [1]

(H) Refer to three aspects: his domineering manner / his appearance (baldness, hard mouth, dark set eyes) / his voice [3]

(I) three [1]

(J) Refer to the understanding of *vessels* being something that you fill **and** Gradgrind's idea of education being that children should be filled with knowledge (*Facts!*). [2]

(K) Refer to any two: the repetition of the word *Facts!* / the use of capitalisation for F / the exclamation mark [2]

Unit 2

(A) All correctly matched for 1 mark: *belief / custom* [2]

(B) unusual [1]

(C) Refer to both the employment of sailors in theatres and the significance of whistling for them leading to incorrect movement of the set and fly system. [2]

(D) Refer to any three points: safety curtain / fire officer if real flames used / electric lights not gas lamps with flames / better design of entrances and exits [3]

(E) 1 mark for each: *tragic loss of life / catastrophic fire devastated …* [2]

(F) 1 mark for each: so that ghosts can perform / to stop last person in theatre tripping over set in the dark [2]

(G) All correct for 1 mark: Fact, Opinion, Fact, Opinion [1]

(H) Complete table = 3 marks; any 3-4 correct = 2 marks; 2 correct = 1 mark

Blue: expensive so worn to hide the fact a company was not doing well

No more than two lit candles: Fire safety

Yellow and green: associated with the devil

Flowers: will die

Mirrors: interfere with lighting [3]

(I) For the full 3 marks, refer to a range of the superstitions and link them to either history or safety. Historical origins:

Whistling/sailors being employed in theatres in the past

Candles/before electric light

Colours/historical associations or costs

Safety:

Whistling/sailors – falling set

Candles/lack of electric light meant naked flames used

Ghost light/tripping hazards in the dark [3]

Unit 3

(A) to fly (on a chair) using helium balloons [1]

(B) Include the narrator's view and his colleagues, for both marks: e.g. he (the narrator) keeps thinking about it and takes it seriously but the others don't take it seriously [2]

(C) Lifted off the ground [1]

(D) 1 mark for any one: *as children / most of us / crosses cultures and borders* [1]

(E) Refer to three of the following: gaining licence at flight school / calculating number of balloons / designing it (*rigging and safety harness*) / working out how it would fly (*physics*) on paper / building models [3]

(F) first [1]

(G) All correctly matched for 1 mark: Number of balloons lifting the chair = 55 / Distance travelled in four hours = 50 miles / Length of world record-breaking flight = 14 hours / Height above the ground reached = 15 000 feet. [1]

(H) 1 mark for any one: He wasn't not just interested in breaking records / he was just trying to prove he could do it. [1]

(I) For 2 marks refer to the literal meaning (being able to physically reach something) and how it is being used figuratively here, indicating he is close to being able to reach his goal. [2]

(J) Refer to the following for 2 marks: the *cluster of balloons* being an unusual aircraft; the word *approaching* suggesting the narrator was nervous or doing something out of the ordinary, which the authorities may disagree with. [2]

(K) 1 mark for each: *not a reckless adventurer / had planned scrupulously* [2]

(L) 1 mark for each: the view of the cliffs of Dover (land disappearing) / the silence. [2]

(M) He had thought of all the possible difficulties. [1]

(N) 1 mark for each: he didn't have permission to land in Belgium / the wires between the towers could cut through his balloons. [2]

(O) Refer to any three of the following, in order: curiosity to begin with / determination to try it / careful and well prepared / fear the night before / relief when he was airborne / enjoyment (delight in flight) / sense of achievement at end. [3]

Unit 4

(A) 1 mark for each of any two: her boredom (*tired of sitting…having nothing to do*) / her indolence (*worth the trouble*) / her preference for picture books (*what is the use of a book…*) / her sleepiness in the heat (*the hot day made her…*). [2]

(B) 1 mark for each of any two: rabbit speaking / rabbit has a watch which he looks at / rabbit is wearing a waistcoat. [2]

(C) Suddenly realised something [1]

(D) 1 mark each: *burning with curiosity* shows Alice is dying to find out more about the rabbit and where he has gone / She shows this by following him down the rabbit hole and not thinking about how she will get out. [2]

(E) 1 mark for each of any two: it is described as very deep or taking long time to fall / the words *down, down, down* are repeated twice / she has time to think and pick things up from the shelves as she falls / she wonders if it will ever end / she refers to coming out the other side of the earth which is obviously exaggerated but emphasises the depth. [2]

(F) *to her disappointment it was empty* [1]

(G) Refer to both the well (1 mark) and Alice's thoughts (2 marks): the slightly bizarre description of the walls of the well: it is described as having cupboards and bookshelves which we would not usually associate with a well / it also has maps and pictures which again would not usually be on the walls of a tunnel. Also, although it is described as *dark*, this is not frightening for Alice.

Also refer to Alice's thoughts/inferred feelings: she does not appear to be worried – it describes her having time to think. The author also included several passages where Alice's thoughts are described in detail (*thought Alice to herself*). She even has chance to think about what others will say when she goes home. Answers may mention the humorous tone as she describes falling through the earth. [3]

(H) 1 mark each for any two: Alice refers to the depth of the earth (*Alice had learnt several things of this sort in her*

lessons…) / she has heard of latitude and longitude but doesn't seem to know what they are / she can't remember the word for 'Antipodes' but thinks it is *The Antipathies* which suggests she was taught the word and knows roughly what it should sound like. [2]

(I) Suggests Alice is sad (disappointed) the key doesn't work [1]

(J) All correct for 1 mark: False, True, True, False [1]

(K) The main changes in her feelings should be outlined for 3 marks: starts off bored and fed up, then feels curious as she sees the White Rabbit, while she is falling and when she lands, then she feels sad when she can't open the doors and wonders how she'll get out. Finally, she ends up delighted and happy because the key works. [3]

(L) For 3 marks, refer fully to both key words in the title, with evidence: adventure (Alice following the rabbit, falling, going to a strange place, exploring hidden passages and trying to get through locked doors); Wonderland (unusual sights such as the shelves and cupboards, a talking rabbit in a waistcoat, the little keys and tiny door) – these all suggest a kind of fantasy land. For answers which refer to both aspects but give limited evidence for each, award 2 marks. For one aspect only, award 1 mark. [3]

(M) All elements in the correct order for 1 mark: Alice spots the White Rabbit above ground. The White Rabbit disappears down a rabbit hole under the hedge. Alice finds a marmalade jar. Alice thinks about her cat. Alice finds a small key. [1]

Unit 5

(A) Two reasons for 2 marks: it is winter – cold weather, therefore no berries to eat and needs a place to stay / bird in story has a broken wing – other birds can fly to warmer places. [2]

(B) Table completed with relevant quotes from text:
Birch: *beautiful, fair green leaves, not very strong*
Oak: *strong, great*. [1]

(C) The oak is only worried about itself (and its own acorns) and is horrified at the idea of the bird's request. [1]

(D) 1 mark each for any two: She draws herself up proudly / She doesn't want to speak to the bird / She tells it to leave her alone. [2]

(E) Refer to either the bird feeling sad (inferred from *poor little bird* and the fact all the others have gone) or uncertain (worried) (inferred from *did not know what to do* and trying to fly with broken wing). [1]

(F) 1 mark for each tree: Spruce: provided home in her branches / Pine: sheltered bird and spruce from wind / Juniper: provided berries [3]

(G) on her branches [1]

(H) Refer to the figurative nature of the description: trees are given human characteristics and people might pull their clothes in around them if they want to draw themselves away from someone else. [1]

(I) playful and lively [1]

(J) 1 mark for each of the five features mentioned in the text box, with evidence from the story:

Characters are usually animals or humans: main character is a bird who can speak.

Moral or message: story is all about being kind to those in need and not turning others away. The trees who do not help are 'punished' by losing their leaves.

Things in threes: the trees feature in two groups of three.

Explain how something came into being: how evergreens got to keep their leaves.

A quest or challenge: the bird is trying to solve the challenge of being left in a cold place for winter.

Magic powers: the frost king commands the wind.

Good over evil: the bird survives; the kind trees are spared losing their leaves. [5]

Unit 6

(A) *is married to* or *(in an alliance) planned (to…)* [1]

(B) A queen in the 1100s would mean the wife of a king, not someone who ruled in their own right. [1]

(C) *apparently* [1]

(D) for both marks, refer to both disorder and lack of stable rule: for example, countryside is plundered, fighting, barons taking control of some places, systems breaking down such as barons making their own coins. [2]

(E) Refer to both aspects: power – barons wanted power and this was shown by them taking control in some places; greedy – they took advantage of the war to get something for themselves. [2]

(F) Refer to both aspects: bravery – shown by scaling the wall on a rope, or attempting to escape when the castle is besieged by herself enemy / clever – shown by wearing disguise to camouflage herself against the snow. [2]

(G) Only the first two should be circled: Neither side making progress. Her son taking over her campaign. [1]

(H) Refer to all three aspects: *great* – her being born the daughter of a king / *Greater by marriage* – her marriages to powerful and important men in Europe meant she gained more status / *Greatest in her offspring* – her son (offspring) went on to become King of England and win the fight she had started for her line to continue on the throne. [3]

(I) Refer to her fight to rule as Queen of England in her own right, as a king would be able to. For more simplistic

answers (for example, 'she wanted to be like a king') only award 1 mark. [2]

(J) Refer three aspects with evidence for full marks, inferring her character from the text. Possible responses: determined (evidence = came to England to fight for her right; did not give up when besieged in the castle) / ambitious (evidence = fought to rule even though at the time, daughters of kings did not become queens) / brave/ courageous (evidence = dangerous castle escape; staying in England and fighting her cause in civil war) / arrogant (evidence = reports of her being arrogant and haughty) / clever (evidence = came up with a plan to escape; advised her son when he was King). Any other plausible characteristics with appropriate supporting evidence. [3]

Unit 7

(A) *famous* [1]

(B) Refer to personification of the city like someone wearing beautiful clothes. [1]

(C) Refer to any three aspects: ships / tops of buildings like churches, theatres and temples (towers, domes)/ fields in the distance / the sky / the river [3]

(D) *silent / asleep / still* [3]

(E) the river is flowing gently / it is not rushing / it can go where it wants. [1]

(F) All correct for 1 mark: False, False, True, True [1]

(G) calm, peaceful [1]

(H) All correctly matched for 1 mark: The houses = Are so quiet they seem to be asleep / Buildings in the city = Sparkle and shine in the morning sun / The River Thames = Flows gently / The view of London = Has impressive beauty. [1]

(I) 1 mark each: Refer to the city being big (*mighty*) / the busy centre of the city is quiet in the morning [2]

(J) Answers should refer to him writing about his own experience (as shown by the title; references to his feelings and opinions of the view of London) / usually writing about nature – in the poem he compares the city to other beautiful things including nature and suggests the city is more beautiful. [2]

(K) Refer to any two examples of plausible evidence of beauty from the poem, including quotations: e.g. *a sight so touching / majesty / wear The beauty of the morning / All bright and glittering / Never did a sun more beautifully steep.* etc. [2]

Unit 8

 (A) *mortal* [1]

(B) He is too weak to lift his head properly. [1]

(C) Refer to two of the following: running to the man / they try to help him up / sharing their food (even though they do not have much). [2]

(D) Refer to all three actions: take one of the three paths each / find the house at the end / buy the first thing that they see there. [3]

(E) Table correctly completed for 1 mark:

Raincoat = Will take you wherever you wish to go.

Book = Tells you what is going on in all parts of the world.

Bottle of liquid = Brings the dead back to life. [1]

(F) Diego thinks he has got something amazing (better than his companions). [1]

(G) Because the princess has already died and black is the colour of mourning. [1]

(H) Refer to any two of the following: they entered the church boldly, when everyone else was upset about the princess / they were not wearing mourning clothes (were wearing red) / they were unknown / they claimed the princess was not dead. [2]

(I) escorted [1]

(J) He was afraid of what might happen if he had failed. [1]

(K) bewildered [1]

(L) Refer to any two of the following: Juan does not deserve to marry her because he did not acknowledge the help of the other two / the other two do not deserve to marry her because they complained instead of accepting their misfortune quietly / he showed the men where to get the three magic items which saved her / he gave them the money to buy the items. [2]

(M) All correctly matched for 1 mark:

Action = he continued to hold the bottle under the nose of the princess

Description of character = Her cheeks were as fresh and rosy as ever

A past event = had been transformed by a wizard into an old man [1]

Unit 9

(A) *loveliest* [1]

(B) White blossom on the tree makes it look as if it has white clothes on at Easter time. [1]

(C) Refer to two of the following aspects: the impression of beauty the poet creates by describing the tree *hung with bloom* / personification of the cherry tree: *stands... Wearing white* [2]

(D) the poet's age [1]

(E) In blossom [1]

(F) Answers should refer to three of the following:

next door's garden / flowers / places he's never seen / a river / dusty roads (with people going to town) [3]

(G) The river looks blue because it is reflecting the blue of the sky. [1]

(H) Answers could refer to any two: *little* me / refers to places *that I had never seen* / refers to *fairy land* which is childlike / dreams of a place where toys come alive. [2]

(I) Refer to the metaphorical meaning, for example 'Because it is about places which seem like foreign places from the child's point of view'. [1]

(J) The widest part of the river that meets the sea/the estuary. [1]

Unit 10

(A) dirty [1]

(B) Refer to any three of the following aspects: his unkempt appearance / his physical stature / his experience, as shown by the scars / his gruff manner, as shown by the way he addresses the narrator's father. [3]

(C) 1 mark for each: He goes to the cliffs and looks out to sea with a telescope by day. / He sits by the fire in the inn and drinks rum by night. [2]

(D) He wants to steer clear of a particular sailor. [1]

(E) He keeps a look out for particular sailor with one leg whom the captain is afraid of. [1]

(F) Refer to two of the following: Coming on stormy nights / having horrible expressions / like a monster / leg cut off in different places / chases him. [2]

(G) 1 mark for each: The narrator thinks the stories are a good thing and that people like them, because they liven up the usually quiet place / His father thinks they put people off coming to the inn because they are afraid. [2]

(H) Refer to any three options with evidence:

His appearance and manner is intriguing to the narrator as shown by the detailed description.

His attraction for people coming to the inn.

He pays the narrator so he perhaps looks up to him.

His appearance and manner is so horrible it might upset the narrator, even though he knows it attracts customers.

He has nightmares about the one-legged man.

He says he *remembers him as if were yesterday*, so it has obviously had a big impact on him. [3]

G The birch tree says that she does not want a strange bird... [1]

Tick **one**.

eating her berries ☐

amongst her leaves ☐

on her branches ☐

taking her acorns ☐

H *the three trees drew their leaves closely about them.*

Explain why this description is effective. [1]

_____

_____

I The word *frolic*, towards the end of the story, suggests the wind is: [1]

Circle **one**.

cold and damp

powerful and strong

wild and fast

playful and lively

J Explain why this story is a good example of a folk tale. **Refer to the whole text and the definition** of a folk tale in your answer. [5]

_____

_____

_____

_____

_____

8

The Queen Who Wanted to be King

Read the text below, then answer the questions that follow.

1102: England is ruled by King Henry I, youngest son of William the Conqueror. His wife, Queen Matilda, gives birth to a daughter – also called Matilda.

1114: The twelve-year-old Matilda is married to the Holy Roman Emperor and King of Germany, Henry V – a man over twice her age, in an alliance planned to strengthen political and royal bonds within Europe. **5**

1120: Matilda's brother and heir to the English throne dies at sea, leaving Matilda the only legitimate child of King Henry I. Unfortunately for Matilda, at this point in history the title 'Queen' refers only to the wife of a king: the idea of a queen ruling in her own right is unprecedented. Nevertheless, in the years that follow, King Henry I persuades the powerful nobles of the English court to swear **10** allegiance to Matilda as his successor upon his death.

1128: Matilda remarries, this time to a man 11 years her junior, Geoffrey of Anjou, a French nobleman. Again the marriage is a political match, intended to secure peace within France, between Normandy and Anjou.

1135: Henry I dies whilst in France, apparently from food poisoning caused by **15** eating too many eels. His death leaves a power vacuum, since the English nobles are reluctant to support a female monarch, despite their earlier pledge to the late King.

1135: Matilda's cousin, Stephen, seizes the English throne, with the backing of the church.

1139: Matilda returns to England to claim her right to the crown. She is given the **20** title 'Lady of England and Normandy' and a date is planned for her coronation. Matilda is never crowned however. Sources suggest Matilda's haughty manner does not go down well with some powerful noblemen and churchmen and some change allegiances. Her quest for the throne divides public opinion and civil war breaks out. The war would go on to last for 19 years and becomes known as 'The **25** Anarchy'. The countryside is plundered, fighting takes place between rival forces and Stephen is captured, although he is eventually released. Power-greedy barons use the opportunity to their advantage, taking control in some parts of England and even minting their own coins. England is in disarray.

1142: Matilda is captured and is besieged in Oxford Castle. **_Legend_** has it the **30** brave and clever Matilda evades her captors by descending the castle walls with ropes and escaping, wearing white to camouflage herself against the snow and running across the frozen river to safety.

1148: After years of stalemate, Matilda returns to France. She is not defeated, however: although her own battle to reign is lost, her eldest son, also called Henry, continues to pursue his family's right the throne, campaigning to become the future king and eventually engineering a successful compromise. **35**

1154: The Treaty of Westminster, an official document, is signed by Stephen and Henry, Matilda's son, in which it is agreed that Stephen remains in power until his death, at which point Henry succeeds him, becoming King Henry II of England. Matilda acts as his advisor and representative in Normandy until her death. **40**

1167: Matilda dies, a queen but never crowned. Her epitaph, written in Latin, translates as:

Great by birth, Greater by marriage, Greatest in her offspring.

by Christine Jenkins **45**

(A) In the section of text for 1114, which word or phrase shows that her marriage was not something she had any control over? [1]

_____

(B) Explain how the title of Queen differs from the modern understanding. [1]

_____

(C) In the text for 1135, which word suggests that the evidence for the King's cause of death may not be certain? [1]

_____

(D) The Oxford English Dictionary defines the term 'anarchy' as a 'state of disorder due to absence of authority or law'. Explain why 'The Anarchy' is a suitable name for the civil war in this text. [2]

_____

_____

(E) Explain why *power-greedy* is an effective choice of word to describe the barons. [2]

_____

_____

7

(F) *the brave and clever Matilda*

How does her escape from Oxford Castle demonstrate that Matilda was *brave and clever*? [2]

(G) In 1148, Matilda left England due to… [1]

Circle **all** those which are true.

Neither side making progress.

Her son taking over her campaign.

King Stephen winning.

Her losing interest in the war.

(H) *Great by birth, Greater by marriage, Greatest in her offspring.*

Explain what is meant by the words on Matilda's epitaph and give reasons why they effectively summarise her life. [3]

(I) Explain why the title *The Queen Who Wanted to be King* is an appropriate one, using evidence from across the text. [2]

(J) Based on what you have read, what impression do we get of Matilda's character? Use evidence from across the text to support your answer. [3]

Composed Upon Westminster Bridge

Read through the poem twice and answer the questions that follow.

> William Wordsworth (1770–1850) was a famous poet who lived around 200 years ago. Born in the beautiful Lake District, he grew up with a deep love of nature and many of his poems reflected this. He also frequently included his own experiences in his poems. In the poem below, Wordsworth wrote about the view from Westminster Bridge across the River Thames, which he witnessed one morning on a visit to London.

Composed Upon Westminster Bridge, September 3, 1802

Earth has not anything to show more fair:

Dull would he be of soul who could pass by

A sight so touching in its majesty:

This City now doth, like a garment, wear

The beauty of the morning; silent, bare,   5

Ships, towers, domes, theatres, and temples lie

Open unto the fields, and to the sky;

All bright and glittering in the smokeless air.

Never did sun more beautifully steep

In his first splendour, valley, rock, or hill;   10

Ne'er saw I, never felt, a calm so deep!

The river glideth at his own sweet will:

Dear God! the very houses seem asleep;

And all that mighty heart is lying still!

By William Wordsworth

(A) In the introductory paragraph, which word shows that Wordsworth is well known? [1]

_____

(B) *This City now doth, like a garment, wear*

   The beauty of the morning

   Explain how these lines in the poem use language effectively to describe the city. [1]

_____

_____

(C) Describe the sight that the poet can see as he stands on the bridge. [3]

_____

_____

_____

(D) Find and copy **three** words in the poem which suggest the city is quiet at this time of day. [3]

_____

(E) *The river glideth at his own sweet will*

   What impression of the river does this line create? [1]

_____

(F) Tick whether the following statements about the poem are true or false. [1]

	True	False
The early-morning air in London was polluted.		
London has many valleys and hills.		
The sun was just rising.		
Beyond the city was the countryside.		

10

ⓖ How does the sight of the city make Wordsworth feel? [1]

_____

8

ⓗ Match the description to the things that they describe. [1]

The houses		Has impressive beauty
Buildings in the city		Flows gently
The River Thames		Sparkle and shine in the morning sun
The view of London		Are so quiet they seem to be asleep

ⓘ *And all that mighty heart is lying still!*

What does this line suggest about the city? [2]

_____

_____

ⓙ The introductory paragraph mentions **two** things which Wordsworth often wrote about. Do you think this poem reflects these things well? Explain your views fully, **using evidence from the text**. [2]

_____

_____

_____

ⓚ What evidence is there in the poem that London in the morning is a beautiful place? **Refer to words and phrases from the poem** which help build up this impression. [2]

_____

_____

_____

8

The Legend of Prince Oswaldo

One moonlit night, three young men were walking along a lonely country road. No one knew where they had come from; no one knew where they were going. After a while they came to a place where the road branched into three. They stopped there, wondering which path to take. At this crossroads lay a helpless old man, groaning as if in mortal pain. At the sight of the travellers he tried to raise his head, but in vain. The three companions ran towards him, helped him up and shared some of their meagre supply of rice with him. 5

The sick old man gradually regained his strength, and at last could speak to them. He thanked them, gave each of the companions a hundred pesos, and said, "Each one of you shall take one of these branch-roads. At the end of it is a house where they are selling something. With these hundred pesos that I am giving each of you, you shall buy the first thing that you see there." The three youths accepted the money, and promised to obey the old man's directions. 10

Pedro, who took the left branch, soon came to the house described by the old man. The owner of the house was selling a raincoat. "How much does the coat cost?" Pedro asked the landlord. 15

"One hundred pesos, no more, no less."

"Of what value is it?" said Pedro.

"It will take you wherever you wish to go." So Pedro paid the price, took the raincoat and returned. 20

Diego, who took the middle road, arrived at another house. The owner of this house was selling a book. "How much does your book cost?" Diego inquired of the owner.

"One hundred pesos, no more, no less."

"Of what value is it?" 25

"It will tell you what is going on in all parts of the world." So Diego paid the price, took the book and returned.

Juan, who took the third road, reached yet another house. The owner of the house was selling a bottle that contained some violet-coloured liquid. "How much does the bottle cost?" said Juan. 30

"One hundred pesos, no more, no less."

"Of what value is it?"

"It brings the dead back to life," was the answer. Juan paid the price, took the bottle and returned.

The three travellers met again in the same place where they had separated, but the old man was now nowhere to be found. The first to tell of his adventure was Diego. "Oh, see what I have!" he boasted to his companions. "It tells everything that is going on in the world. Let me show you!" He opened the book and read what appeared on the page: "'The beautiful princess of Berengena is dead. Her parents, relatives and friends grieve at her loss.'" 35

"Good!" answered Juan. "Then there is an occasion for us to test this bottle. It restores the dead back to life. Oh, but the kingdom of Berengena is far away! The princess will be long buried before we get there." 40

"Then we shall have occasion to use my raincoat," said Pedro. "It will take us wherever we wish to go. Let us try it! We shall receive a big reward from the king. We shall return home with a *casco* full of money. To Berengena at once!" He wrapped the raincoat about all three of them, and made a wish. Within a few minutes they reached the country of Berengena. The princess was already in the church, where her parents were grieving over her. The church was full of people weeping, dressed in their black mourning clothes. 45

When the three strangers boldly entered the church, the guard at the door arrested them, for they had on red clothes. When Juan protested, and said that the princess was not dead, the guard immediately took him to the king. The king, when he heard what Juan had said, called him a fool. 50

"She is only sleeping," said Juan. "Let me wake her up!" 55

"She is dead," answered the king angrily. "On your life, don't you dare touch her!"

"I will hold my head responsible for the truth of my statement," said Juan. "Let me wake her up, or rather, not to offend your Majesty, restore her to life!"

"Well, I will let you do as you please," said the king, "but if your attempt fails, you will lose your head. On the other hand, should you be successful, I will give you the princess for a wife, and you shall be my heir." 60

"Everybody here present is to bear witness that I, the King of Berengena, do hereby confirm this agreement with this unknown stranger."

The announcement having been made, Juan was conducted to the coffin. Suddenly he realised what he was undertaking. What if the bottle were false? What if he should fail? His head be dangling from the ropes of the scaffold, to be hailed by the multitude as a fool. The coffin was opened. With these thoughts in his mind, Juan tremblingly uncorked his bottle of violet liquid, and held it under the nose of the princess. He held the bottle there for some time, but she gave no signs of life. He waited. An hour later, still no trace of life. After hours of waiting, the people began to grow impatient. The king scratched his head; the guards were ready to seize him.

65

70

"Nameless stranger," thundered the king, with indignant eyes, "upon your honour, tell us the truth! Can you do it, or not? Speak. I command it!"

Juan trembled all the more. He did not know what to say, but he continued to hold the bottle under the nose of the princess. Had he not been afraid of the consequences, he would have given up and entreated the king for mercy. He fixed his eyes on the corpse, but did not speak. "Are you trying to play a trick on us?" said the king, his eyes flashing with rage. "Speak! I command!"

75

Just as Juan was about to reply, he saw the right hand of the princess move. He bade the king wait. Soon the princess moved her other hand and opened her eyes. Her cheeks were as fresh and rosy as ever. She stared about, and exclaimed in surprise, "Oh, where am I? Where am I? Am I dreaming? No, there is my father, there is my mother, there is my brother." The king was fully satisfied. He embraced his daughter, and then turned to Juan, saying, "Stranger, will you now tell us your name?"

80

85

As politely as he could, Juan replied to the king, told his name, and said that he was a poor labourer from far away. The king only smiled, and ordered Juan's clothes to be exchanged for prince's garments, so that the celebration of his marriage with the princess might take place at once. "Long live Juan! Long live the princess!" the people shouted.

90

When Diego and Pedro heard the shout, they could not help feeling cheated. They made their way through the crowd, and said to the king, "Great Majesty, pray hear us! In the name of justice, pray hear us!"

"Who calls?" asked the king. "Bring him here!" A guard led the two men before the king.

95

"What is the matter?" asked the king.

"Your Majesty," responded Diego. "If it had not been for my book, we could not have known that the princess was dead. Our home is far away, and it was only because of my magic book that we knew of the events that were going on here."

"And his Majesty shall be informed," seconded Pedro, "that Juan's good luck   100
is due to my raincoat. Neither Diego's book nor Juan's bottle could have done
anything had not my raincoat carried us here so quickly. I am the one who
should marry the princess."

The king was confounded. Each of the three had a good reason, but all three
could not marry the princess. Even the king's advisors could not agree on the   105
matter.

While they were puzzling over it, an old man sprang forth from the crowd and
declared that he would settle the difficulty. "Young men," he said, addressing
Juan, Pedro and Diego, "none of you shall marry the princess. You, Juan, shall
not marry her, because you intended to obtain your fortunes regardless of your   110
companions who have been helping you to get them. And you, Pedro and Diego,
shall not have the princess, because you did not accept your misfortune quietly
and thank God for it. None of you shall have her. I will marry her myself."

The princess wept. How could the fairest maiden of Berengena marry an old man?
"What right have you to claim her?" said the king in scorn.   115

"I am the one who showed these three companions where to get their bottle,
raincoat and book," said the old man. "I am the one who gave each of them a
hundred pesos."

The old man was right. The crowd clapped their hands; and the princess could do
nothing but yield. Bitterly weeping, she gave her hand to the old man and they   120
were married by the priest.

The newly-married couple were led from the altar to be taken home to the
palace, but, just as they were descending the steps, the whole church was
flooded with light. All present were dazzled, but the glorious illumination did not
last long. When the people recovered, they found that their princess was walking   125
not with an old man, but a gallant young prince. The king recognized him. The
king's new son-in-law was none other than Prince Oswaldo, who had just been
set free from the bonds of enchantment by his marriage. He had been a former
suitor of the princess, but had been transformed by a wizard into an old man.
With magnificent ceremony the king's son-in-law was seated on the throne, and   130
he was hailed as King Oswaldo of Berengena.

A traditional Filipino tale, adapted by Christine Jenkins

(A) Look at the first paragraph. Find and copy **one** word which shows that the old man seemed to be dying. [1]

(B) *At the sight of the travellers he tried to raise his head, but in vain.*

What do the words *in vain* suggest about the old man in the first paragraph? Tick **one**. [1]

He does not bother to lift his head.

He lifts his head but the travellers are out of sight.

He is too weak to lift his head properly.

He does not want any fuss from the travellers.

(C) What evidence is there in the first paragraph that the three young men are kind? [2]

(D) In the paragraph beginning *The sick old man gradually regained his strength...*, what instructions does the old man give the three companions? [3]

(E) Complete the table below, filling in the **three** items purchased by the young men and their magical powers. [1]

Item	Magical powers

(F) Look at the paragraph beginning *The three travellers met again...*

What does the word *boasted* suggest about Diego's opinion of what he bought? [1]

9

Ⓖ Why were people dressed in black when the three companions arrived? [1]

Ⓗ Read the paragraph beginning *When the three strangers boldly entered the church...*

Give **two** reasons why the strangers may have stood out when they entered the church. [2]

Ⓘ In the paragraph beginning *The announcement having been made...*, which word most closely matches the meaning of the word *conducted*? Circle **one**. [1]

given   escorted   welcomed   directed

Ⓙ Why did Juan not beg the king for mercy? [1]

Ⓚ In the paragraph beginning *The king was confounded...*, what does the word *confounded* mean? Circle **one**. [1]

delighted   angry   uneasy   bewildered

Ⓛ According to the old man, why does he deserve to marry the princess more than any of the three companions? [2]

Ⓜ Draw lines to match the part of the story to the quotation. [1]

| Action | | had been transformed by a wizard into an old man |

| Description of character | | he continued to hold the bottle under the nose of the princess |

| A past event | | Her cheeks were as fresh and rosy as ever |

9

Cherry Trees

The two poems below are both about cherry trees. Read them each through twice and answer the questions that follow.

Loveliest of Trees, the Cherry Now

Loveliest of trees, the cherry now
Is hung with bloom along the bough,
And stands about the woodland ride
Wearing white for Eastertide.

Now, of my threescore years and ten,   5
Twenty will not come again,
And take from seventy springs a score,*
It only leaves me fifty more.

And since to look at things in bloom
Fifty springs are little room,   10
About the woodlands I will go
To see the cherry hung with snow.

By A. E. Housman

*a score means 20 of something

In the second verse of this poem, 'threescore years and ten' refers to the age of 70,
which was the average life expectancy at the time.

Foreign Lands

Up into the cherry tree
Who should climb but little me?
I held the trunk with both my hands
And looked abroad in foreign lands.

I saw the next door garden lie,   5
Adorned with flowers, before my eye,
And many pleasant places more
That I had never seen before.

I saw the dimpling river pass
And be the sky's blue looking-glass;   10
The dusty roads go up and down
With people tramping in to town.

If I could find a higher tree
Farther and farther I should see,
To where the grown-up river slips   15
Into the sea among the ships,

To where the roads on either hand
Lead onward into fairy land,
Where all the children dine at five,
And all the playthings come alive.   20

From *A Child's Garden of Verses* by Robert Louis Stevenson

Ⓐ Look at the poem 'Loveliest of Trees, the Cherry Now'.

Which word in the first verse of this poem shows that the poet thinks the cherry is the best tree? [1]

_____

Ⓑ *Wearing white for Eastertide*

What is the poet describing in this line? [1]

_____

Ⓒ What impression of the cherry tree does the poet create in the first verse? [2]

_____

_____

Ⓓ What is revealed in verse two? Tick **one**. [1]

| The time of year | ☐ | The poet's age | ☐ |
| The time of day | ☐ | The age of the cherry tree | ☐ |

5

(E) In the third verse, the poet wants to go and see the tree while it is: Tick **one**. [1]

Covered in snow ☐   In blossom ☐

With bare branches ☐   Hanging with cherries ☐

(F) Look at the poem called 'Foreign Lands'.

Write down **three** things the poet can see when he climbs the cherry tree. [3]

_____

_____

_____

(G) *I saw the dimpling river pass*

And be the sky's blue looking-glass

Explain what this description tells us about the river. [1]

_____

(H) This poem is written from the viewpoint of a child. How does the poet create this impression? **Refer to words and phrases from the poem** in your answer. [2]

_____

_____

(I) Why is the title 'Foreign Lands' an effective one? [1]

_____

_____

(J) Look at the lines *To where the grown-up river slips, Into the sea among the ships*

What is being described? [1]

_____

9

The Old Buccaneer

Read the text below, then answer the questions that follow.

I remember him as if it were yesterday, as he came plodding to the inn door, his sea-chest following behind him in a hand-barrow; a tall, strong, heavy, nut-brown man; his tarry pigtail falling over the shoulders of his soiled blue coat; his hands ragged and scarred, with black, broken nails, and the sabre cut across one cheek, a dirty, livid white. I remember him looking round the cove and whistling   **5**
to himself as he did so, and then breaking out in that old sea song that he sang so often afterwards:

"Fifteen men on the dead man's chest,
Yo-ho-ho and a bottle of rum!"

in the high, old tottering voice that seemed to have been tuned and broken at   **10**
the capstan bars. Then he rapped on the door with a bit of stick like a handspike that he carried, and when my father appeared, called roughly for a glass of rum. This, when it was brought to him, he drank slowly, like a connoisseur, lingering on the taste, and still looking about him at the cliffs and up at our signboard.

"This is a handy cove," says he, at length; "and a pleasant sittyated [situated]   **15**
grog-shop. Much company, mate?"

My father told him no, very little company, the more was the pity.

"Well, then," said he, "this is the berth for me. Here you, matey," he cried to the man who trundled the barrow; "bring up alongside and help up my chest. I'll stay here a bit," he continued. "I'm a plain man; rum and bacon and eggs is   **20**
what I want, and that head up there for to watch ships off. What you mought [might] call me? You mought call me captain. Oh, I see what you're at—there"; and he threw down three or four gold pieces on the threshold. "You can tell me when I've worked through that," said he, looking as fierce as a commander.

And, indeed, bad as his clothes were, and coarsely as he spoke, he had none of   **25**
the appearance of a man who sailed before the mast, but seemed like a mate or skipper, accustomed to be obeyed or to strike. The man who came with the barrow told us the mail had set him down the morning before at the Royal George; that he had inquired what inns there were along the coast, and hearing ours well spoken of, I suppose, and described as lonely, had chosen it from the   **30**
others for his place of residence. And that was all we could learn of our guest.

He was a very silent man by custom. All day he hung round the cove, or upon the cliffs, with a brass telescope; all evening he sat in a corner of the parlour next the fire, and drank rum and water very strong. Mostly he would not speak when spoken to; only look up sudden and fierce, and blow through his nose like a fog- **35** horn; and we and the people who came about our house soon learned to let him be. Every day, when he came back from his stroll, he would ask if any seafaring men had gone by along the road. At first we thought it was the want of company of his own kind that made him ask this question; but at last we began to see he was desirous to avoid them. When a seaman put up at the Admiral Benbow (as **40** now and then some did, making by the coast road for Bristol), he would look in at him through the curtained door before he entered the parlour; and he was always sure to be as silent as a mouse when any such was present. For me, at least, there was no secret about the matter; for I was, in a way, a sharer in his alarms.

He had taken me aside one day and promised me a silver fourpenny on the first **45** of every month if I would only keep my "weather eye open for a seafaring man with one leg," and let him know the moment he appeared. Often enough when the first of the month came round, and I applied to him for my wage, he would only blow through his nose at me, and stare me down; but before the week was out he was sure to think better of it, bring me my fourpenny piece, and repeat **50** his orders to look out for "the seafaring man with one leg."

How that personage haunted my dreams, I need scarcely tell you. On stormy nights, when the wind shook the four corners of the house, and the surf roared along the cove and up the cliffs, I would see him in a thousand forms, and with a thousand diabolical expressions. Now the leg would be cut off at the knee, now at **55** the hip; now he was a monstrous kind of a creature who had never had but one leg, and that in the middle of his body. To see him leap and run and pursue me over hedge and ditch was the worst of nightmares. And altogether I paid pretty dear for my monthly fourpenny piece, in the shape of these abominable fancies.

But though I was so terrified by the idea of the seafaring man with one leg, **60** I was far less afraid of the captain himself than anybody else who knew him. There were nights when he took a deal more rum and water than his head would carry; and then he would sometimes sit and sing his wicked, old, wild sea songs, minding nobody; but sometimes he would call for glasses round, and force all the trembling company to listen to his stories or bear a chorus to his singing. **65** Often I have heard the house shaking with "Yo-ho-ho and a bottle of rum," all the neighbours joining in for dear life, with the fear of death upon them, and each singing louder than the other to avoid remark. For in these fits he was the most overriding companion ever known; he would slap his hand on the table

for silence all around; he would fly up in a passion of anger at a question, or 70
sometimes because none was put, and so he judged the company was not
following his story. Nor would he allow anyone to leave the inn till he had drunk
himself sleepy and reeled off to bed.

His stories were what frightened people worst of all. Dreadful stories they were;
about hanging, and walking the plank, and storms at sea, and the Dry Tortugas, 75
and wild deeds and places on the Spanish Main. By his own account, he must
have lived his life among some of the wickedest men that God ever allowed
upon the sea; and the language in which he told these stories shocked our plain
country people almost as much as the crimes that he described. My father was
always saying the inn would be ruined, for people would soon cease coming 80
there to be tyrannized over and put down and sent shivering to their beds; but
I really believe his presence did us good. People were frightened at the time, but
on looking back they rather liked it; it was a fine excitement in a quiet country
life; and there was even a party of the younger men who pretended to admire
him, calling him a "true sea-dog," and a "real old salt," and such like names, and 85
saying there was the sort of man that made England terrible at sea.

From *Treasure Island* by Robert Louis Stevenson

Ⓐ Look at the first paragraph. The word *soiled* suggests the captain's coat was... Circle **one**. [1]

rough   pale   dirty   ragged

Ⓑ Reread the first paragraph, to the paragraph ending *...at our signboard*.

What impression of the old captain do you get from these paragraphs? [3]

_____

_____

_____

Ⓒ Look at the paragraph beginning *He was a very silent man by custom*.

How does the captain spend his time? [2]

_____

_____

6

D *Every day, when he came back from his stroll, he would ask if any seafaring men had gone by along the road.*

What is the reason the captain asks this question? Tick **one**. [1]

He is lonely and wants some company. ☐

He wants to meet up with some fellow sailors. ☐

He wants to steer clear of a particular sailor. ☐

He wants to go back to sea. ☐

E How does the narrator earn money from the captain? [1]

F Reread the paragraph beginning *How that personage haunted my dreams...*

Give **two** things the narrator dreams about the one-legged sailor. [2]

G Look at the paragraph beginning *His stories were what frightened people worst of all*.

How do the narrator and his father disagree about the captain's stories? [2]

H Do you think the narrator likes having the captain staying at the inn? Tick **one**. Explain your choice fully, using evidence from the text. [3]

Yes ☐

No ☐

Maybe ☐

9

autobiographical: writing which is about the author's own life.

extract: a short passage of text taken from a longer book.

folk tale: a traditional story from a particular culture, usually passed on from person to person.

legend: a traditional story from the past which has been handed down over time and cannot be proved to be true.

moral: a message or meaning which lies behind a story.

narrator: a person who is telling a story.

phrase: a short group of words, which do not form a full sentence on their own.

Progress chart

How did you do? Fill in your score below and shade in the corresponding boxes to compare your progress across the different tests and units.

50%   100%

Unit 1, p4 Score __ / 9

Unit 1, p5 Score __ / 9

Unit 2, p8 Score __ / 10

Unit 2, p9 Score __ / 9

Unit 3, p12 Score __ / 9

Unit 3, p13 Score __ / 10

Unit 3, p14 Score __ / 6

Unit 4, p17 Score __ / 5

Unit 4, p18 Score __ / 11

Unit 4, p19 Score __ / 8

Unit 5, p22 Score __ / 10

50%   100%

Unit 6, p29 Score __ / 7

Unit 6, p30 Score __ / 11

Unit 7, p32 Score __ / 10

Unit 7, p33 Score __ / 8

Unit 8, p38 Score __ / 9

Unit 8, p39 Score __ / 9

Unit 9, p41 Score __ / 5

Unit 9, p42 Score __ / 9

Unit 10, p45 Score __ / 6

Unit 10, p46 Score __ / 9